To Zara, you are my life's greatest joy.
My very own super hero. – J.A.

I'm A Morning Super Hero

Join Zara on her morning adventure, as she uses her powers to master her morning routine. This book encourages parent interaction, participation, and imagination as both parent and child experience the wonders of Zara's morning super powers. Written in a fun style, this book is complemented by visually stunning, large-sized, and full-color illustrations. This is the perfect book to encourage young children to be proactive and steadfast during their morning preparation.

This book provides interaction notes to help the reader and child communicate, connect, and build a lasting experience.

Come join Zara on her daily adventures.

I wake up every morning with a secret beyond your imagination. I have morning super powers.

My super powers help me do amazing things. Let me tell you how!

My parents are amazing. They love my puppy Jimmy and me. Jimmy and I are best friends and together we will save the day.

My powers help me predict what time my parents will get up every morning.

Interaction Notes: Point at the hours on the clock. Do you know what time you wake up in the morning?

I can hear my parents walking down the hallway to my room.

As they open my bedroom door, I picture them saying, "Good morning Zara! It's time to get ready for school," before the words come out of their mouths. My super powers are at it again!

Interaction Notes: What sounds wake you up in the morning? What do you enjoy hearing in the morning?

I have morning super powers! It is amazing having powers that allow me to communicate with my dog, Jimmy.

Jimmy always knows what I am thinking. Just this morning, he retrieved my slippers before I got out of bed. Jimmy to the rescue!

Interaction Notes: What would you like Jimmy to fetch? A book? Toy?

I race to the bathroom and brush my teeth fast and clean. My favorite part of the morning is singing the super brush song.

Interaction Notes: How do you brush your teeth? Pretend to move your toothbrush side to side and up and down.

I help my parents pick my clothes for school every morning.

Interaction Notes: What colors would you like to wear today?
What clothes would you like to wear?

I lay them on the dresser, so I can quickly get dressed and prepared for the day.

It's important to wear clothes that make you feel like a super hero.

Super heroes enjoy eating breakfast in the morning. It helps Jimmy and me stay strong and alert throughout the day.

Interaction Notes: What did Zara eat for breakfast?
What do you like to eat for breakfast?

After breakfast, I like to fly to the school bus stop and greet the driver as I enter the bus. "Good morning," I say.

I protect the students on the bus and make sure there's no bullying. I love being a super hero.

Interaction Notes: How high can you fly? How fast can you fly?

It's great being a super hero.
Until our next adventure – off, off, and away.

Interaction Notes: Wave your hand bye-bye!

I'm a morning super hero!
What super powers do you have in the morning?

_____

_____

_____

_____

_____

_____

_____

_____

_____

_____

_____

_____

_____

_____

I'm A Morning Super Hero

Published by JTZ Books

Company Address: 34 East Germantown Pike, # 251
Norristown, PA 19401

Company Website: JTZBooks.com

ISBN: 978-1-7372739-0-5

Written by Jerry Andre
Cover by Ekaterina Anikina.

Early Children Age 2 - 8

Made in the USA
Middletown, DE
28 February 2023

25829140R00015